ABOUT KILLER APPS

Having another computer or smartphone app that demonstrates a disease to your patient is not a killer app. It may be convenient but not necessary: Here is a definition of a killer app:

kill·er app

noun

informal

a feature, function, or application of a new technology or product that is presented as virtually indispensable or much superior to rival products.

In the many years of lecturing about information technology, my Killer App talk at various meetings has garnered the most interest. I present here the most recent list. I feel that these apps give the user more time, more productivity, and more functionality than other apps out there.

If you feel you have another killer app I am missing then contact me at me though LinkedIn at:

https://www.linkedin.com/in/ira-kirschenbaum-5132001a/

Enjoy!

Ira H. Kirschenbaum, MD

Special Note: Each year, the book is updated. We do this by publishing it in the Spring of each year and keep the same cover but add a sticker noting the year.

About Killer Apps 1

1Password 6

Adobe Acrobat Pro 6

Adobe Acrobat Browser Extension.........................6

Adobe Photography Suite 7

AllTrails 7

Any Free PDF to JPG Converter 8

Amphetamine 8

Apple Music 8

Audible 9

BetterSnapTool 9

Big Talk 10

Bitly 10

Blinkist 10

Burner..11

Canva...11

Calendly...12

Call Recorders (Many)...12

Cam Scanner 13

Camtasia Studio 13

Copy 'Em..13

Delectable..14

Dicom Readers..14

Doc.Social...15

DocuSign 15

Doximity Caller 15

Doxy.me Telehealth 16

Dropbox/Dropbox Business 16

Duolingo 16

eCamm Movie Tools- Call Recorder 17

eqMac Equalizer 17

Encrypto 17

Evernote 17

Expensify 18

Fiverr 18

Flash Card Hero Lite 19

Flipboard 19

F.lux 19

Fresh 20

Giphy 20

Goniometer 20

Google Scholar and Browser Extension 21

Google translate 21

Grammarly 21

HiHello 22

Hotel Tonight 22

Macpaw Hider 2 22

HootSuite 23

Hue 23

iAnnotate 23

ICD10 Consult 24

IMDB 24

iXpand Drive...24

Kahoot 25

Kasa 25

Key Ring 26

LinkedIn 26

MailChimp 26

Measure 27

Monday.com 27

Monosnap 27

multi Copy & Paste 28

multitimer 28

NordVPN 28

Orthopaedicscore.com 29

Pandora..29

Pangea.app 29

Parallels 30

PDF Editor 30

Pocket 30

Podcasts 31

Rakuten 31

Read (QX READ) 31

Reflector 4 32

Shasam 32

Show My Desktop 32

Snagit 33

Spotify 33

Tapt.io 33

Task Rabbit 34

The Score 34

To Do 34

Video Channels- Onliine 35

Vivino 35

VLC 35

Voice Memos 36

Youmail 36

Waze 36

Wondershare MockitT 36

Wundershare Uniconverter 37

World Card 37

X-Mind 37

Zenfolio 38

Zoom 38

1PASSWORD

There are many password managers but this one is a perennial favorite. It, of course, is secure and easy to use. You can not only save passwords but also PIN numbers. The power is that it can autofill sites that require these passwords.

ADOBE ACROBAT PRO

PDF management program. Allows you to convert to other formats edit, sign, and share, and organize PDF documents. A worthwhile investment over the free version all Acrobat Reader. There is even a browser extension that lets you turn any webpage into a PDF.

ADOBE ACROBAT BROWSER EXTENSION

Every browser, Chrome, Edge, or similar, have what are call "extensions." These are add-ons, where the icons live in the right-hand corner of the browser. They are mini programs that enhance certain features of the browser. This particular one for Adobe Acrobat, allows you to convert any webpage you are looking at into an Adobe PDF file. This is very useful when you want to email or use the webpage as a document.

ADOBE PHOTOGRAPHY SUITE

Full-featured photo management and editing. Includes two great applications: 1) Lightroom which is similar to Google's Picasa but incredibly powerful in its ability to keep track of your images and work on them. It also includes the best image editor of all-time- Photoshop. Even if you learn only 1/3 of Photoshop you are way ahead of the game.

ALLTRAILS

First of all, you need to be active and actually want to be outdoors. If you do, then this app is for you. It has over 200,000 trail maps for hiking, running, and biking. Essentially, once you start the app, your phone is a GPS tracker, so it is less likely that you get lost.

ANY FREE PDF TO JPG CONVERTER

For a variety of reasons, such as importing a PDF as an image into a PowerPoint presentation, you may want to convert that PDF into any type of image format. This free app allows you to do that. What is also cool is that it takes each separate page of the PDF and makes a separate image file.

AMPHETAMINE

An app that allows you to set the exact amount of time that you want your computer to go to into sleep mode. Prevents your computer from going into sleep mode until you want it to.

APPLE MUSIC

All the music you will probably ever need. May be a bit pricey for some but integrates with your Apple products incredibly. Non- Apple users- Spotify. There are so superb features. You can, of course,

make as many playlists as you want. Every
Tuesday, Apple Music creates a new playlist from
your library of songs for you based on various
music themes. There is also a custom station,
named after you, that finds all types of songs, new
and old, based on your previous listening patterns.
Additionally, Apple Music creates its own playlists
based on music genre of songs that are no
necessarily in your library.

Audiobooks. Audible, now owned by Amazon, has
nearly every Audiobook on the market. What is
powerful is that when you listen to Audible on your
phone and stop at a point, your iPad, Microsoft
Surface, or computer version of the app picks up
where you left off. A real bargain on cost. You can
also connect your Audible to Waze so when you are
driving it stops when Waze speaks. It also connect
through Apple Car Play and Teslas.

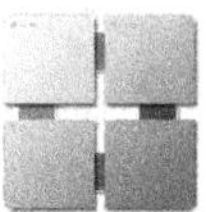

Manage your windows on your desktop. This app
allows you to automatically resize windows on your
desktop for management of multitasking. Can use

quarter screen, half, top, bottom and an array of drag-and-drop sizes of windows.

BIG TALK

The Big Talk Question Card Game helps facilitate in-depth conversations with friends, family members, romantic partners, coworkers, classmates, teammates, community members, and strangers.

BITLY

This is an extension to many web browsers. It allows you to take a very long web address that you want to send to someone and shorten it and even customize it. Now with click tracking.

BLINKIST

Effectively, Blinkist is a massive collection of books summarized in 15-minutes. You can search for a specific book, browse by genre, look at their selections for you, and more. I find it especially good for business books where you are looking for the essence of the book rather than all the examples given. It also allows you information to see if you want to go on and get the full version of the book. Great while you are driving.

BURNER

Own a second phone line without a phone. You get an actual number that is a virtual number on your Smartphone. Relatively inexpensive with no long-term contracts. Some plans start at $5/month.

CANVA

Canva is a massively full-featured design application. It is a total design suite that can be used for documents, presentations, print material, videos, websites, and more. In one fell swoop, you can replace 4-5 different programs that you use to get the total power of Canva. There are a huge number of templates, too.

Stop struggling with people making appointments with you. With Calendly, you can set appointments on your own unique landing page and people can make appointments in those reserved slots. It syncs automatically with your calendar and their calendar. You can even connect it to conferencing apps like GoToMeeting and automatically setup a meeting.

CALL RECORDERS (MANY)

Record incoming and outgoing calls on the fly. This is a game changer! Either before you make a call or after you receive a call you can start this app and the call is recorded. In most states, electronic one-party recording is legal. Check your state laws. According to my most recent search, the following states have adopted some version of two-party consent:
California, Connecticut, Florida, Illinois, Maryland, Massachusetts, Montana, New Hampshire, Pennsylvania and Washington.

A very powerful and useful Smartphone scanner.
You can scan a page of text and aside from copying
this, you can do OCR (optical character
recognition).

CAMTASIA STUDIO

Simple, yet powerful video editing. So much easier
to use than Final Cut (Mac) or Adobe Premier (PC).
Way more powerful than iMovie (Mac). Camtasia
comes in PC and Mac versions. Be your own
YouTube studio!

COPY 'EM

The is a computer-based app that expands your
clipboard capabilities. Usually, well use copy text
or an image, you can only copy one item at a time
to your clipboard. When you copy another item, the
previous item is deleted and you have the new item
in your clipboard. Essentially, the clipboard only

holds one item. Copy 'em is a program that once
you start it allows an unlimited of items to sit in you
clipboard that you can choose from to paste.

DELECTABLE

A wine app similar to another one on this list.
Delectable allows you to personally rate the wines
you place into your virtual cellar after scanning the
label. It does not inform you where you can buy
that wine, though.

DICOM READERS

DICOM reader. My favorite DICOM reader is
Horos. There are a number of DICOM readers out
there. This is one of them. Here are a few others
that Killer Apps audience members have suggested:
MicroDicom, Osirix, PostDicom, RadiAnt.
DICOM is the image standard for x-ray/imaging in
healthcare. The actual images on those CD's you
receive are saved in DICOM format. Having a
DICOM reader is helpful when the programs that
come from the imaging center don't load well or are
made for PC's and you have a Mac.

DOC ☁ SOCIAL

List making tool for Smartphone, tablets, and computers. If you are a list type of person, this is the app for you. Make and share lists on the fly. Even have group lists.

DOCUSIGN

DocuSign®

A secure, document management, cloud-based service. You can upload any documents and develop templates and assign people to fill out of sign different sections.

DOXIMITY CALLER

This is an app within the physician social media site Doximity. It is an app that allows you to call anyone, for example a patient, and change your caller ID. You need to sign up (for free) to Doximity.

The free version of this application is probably all you need to get going in telehealth.

DROPBOX/DROPBOX BUSINESS

Store and share files in the cloud. A great way to store large files or backup files in the cloud and share them with people. You probably know that most email servers don't allow for the transfer of very large files by email, so this is a great way to get this done and have the file stored online for future use. You can also use it to load presentations you are giving just in case you lose your flash drive or have issues with your laptop on the road.

DUOLINGO

Learn a language. A free app that was started by a research team at the University of Pittsburgh that also started Capcha and Recapcha.

Allows you to record Skype conversations.

EQMAC EQUALIZER

When you add this app on your computer you can add an equalizer to customize the sound.

ENCRYPTO

As simple app where you can encrypt any file with a unique password and send the file to someone. You get them the password separately for them to unlock the file.

EVERNOTE

This is the gold-standard of note-taking apps. It syncs across all your devices. Keeps track of tasks and their progress. Also connects with your calendar.

⛟ 🍴 ✈ Expensify

A Smartphone app that connects to your cloud-based app supported by this company that allows you to scan, read, and organize all your expenses when you travel. You simply scan your receipts. The app reads the receipt with optical character recognition and calculates all your expenses. You then produce reports you can see on your Smartphone or computer and send them for processing and payment.

A community of consultants for all kinds of projects from illustrators to editors and more. Sort of like an academic, artistic, and computer geek Task Rabbit. You search for what service you want and a bunch of choice come up for you to hire for your project

Allows you make an unlimited number of flashcards for future reference and study.

FLIPBOARD

News aggregator with flair. This has an entertaining interface to read quite a bit of news posted.

F.LUX

f.lux makes your computer screen look like the room you are in all the time diminishing fatigue.

FRESH

For MacOS. Fresh is essentially the Spotlight
function on turbo. Expands your capability to
search and sort your computer for files and emails.

GIPHY

Allows you to make those cute, animated images
that you can attach to messages to emphasize your
point in any message.

GONIOMETER

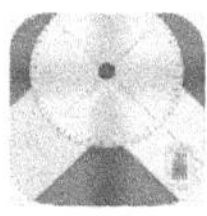

A digital goniometer. Simple, cheap, easy to use.
A lot out there- this is the most basic.

If there is a search term in the Google browser window and you click this extension button, it automatically searched Google Scholar which is rapidly becoming a standard in academic searches.

GOOGLE TRANSLATE

The easiest translator available on the Internet. Multiple languages and also gives you options on which translation to accept with alternate choices. Not a substitute for a professional translation but a good start.

GRAMMARLY

This app, which works on any webpage that you are typing on, corrects your grammar. Free version is great.

A remarkable app that allows you to produce multiple contact cards that you can keep in the app or in the Smartphone wallet so you can share, with a QR code.

HOTEL TONIGHT

Finds lat minute deals in local hotels where you are staying that night.

MACPAW HIDER 2

You can make hidden, encrypted password protected folders on your computer that you can drag any files into.

Allows you to develop posts for multiple social media accounts and time their release.

HUE

Made by Philips, this is a series of million color lighting products that are run by an app on your Smartphone. My favorite is the light strip.

IANNOTATE

PDF Reader for tablets. Reading PDF files on a tablet is easy- editing them and annotating them is not without this app.

ICD10 CONSULT

ICD10 search. There are a lot out there, but this is not only a free one but also maybe the best out there!

IMDB

Huge movie and TV entertainment app. Longtime app about information related to the entertainment industry. I call this a UAR app. UAR stands for Under a Rock- that means that if you are reading this and never heard of this app then you have been living under a rock.

IXPAND DRIVE

SanDisk, the maker of flash drives and more, hit a home run with this combination hardware and software app. It is a flash drive that is attached to your Smartphone and automatically backs up your photos and media. You can choose to delete the media from your phone after transfer or not. Once

you have the data on the flash drive, you can
transfer it easily to your computer.

KAHOOT

This app, which is for computer and smartphone,
allows you, on the fly, to develop surveys for
audience participation for interaction lectures. You
develop the questions and the users connect to the
survey with their smartphones, without
downloading an app and they can answer the
questions and you can then analyze the answers.

KASA

A great Smartphone app that connects to Kasa
switches and outlets to control anything in your
house remotely from your phone. Simple and
inexpensive.

Keeps all loyalty cards on a single app. You no longer have to carry around those annoying loyalty cards or key ring plastics. Just scan in the bar code and it is on file in this app. A vast majority of stores can scan from your phone.

LINKEDIN

The best business-to-business social media site. Start specialty groups and connect to a lot of people in areas of your interest. A huge orthopaedic presence on this social media platform.

MAILCHIMP

Develop mailing lists and send out group emails that can be graphically enhanced. The recipients can opt out. You can include hyperlinks within the email. These can also be scheduled.

MEASURE

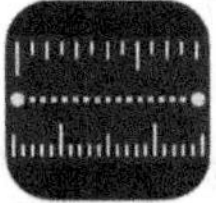

A visual and electronic ruler app installed on your Smartphone.

MONDAY.COM

An easy to use yet powerful project management app for personal or team use. Has the ability to set tasks, deadlines and attach all kinds of files to each item.

MONOSNAP

The easiest and most powerful way to capture or record any part of your computer screen and then edit it, save it, or copy and paste it.

A browser extension that allows you, while typing on any webpage to copy and paste up to three different things and keep ready to paste whichever one you want to.

MULTITIMER

A remarkable timer app where you can time multiple events at once. Great when you are doing time-motion studies for efficiency in the operating room or other places.

NORDVPN

Protected surfing. Whomever you are communicating with on the web does not know your IP address. This is very good. It also may slow down your connection, but I have not found this to be an issue.

This is a site that has a ton of value-based scores such as HOOS, KOOS, DASH, and others. The site allows you to calculate the actual numbers. Truly a labor of love for the web originators of this site. Kudos to them!

PANDORA

Music listening app. Great way to stream music by artist, category, or customize your own group of artists to play them and similar music.

PANGEA.APP

Pangea helps companies find and hire college students for freelance jobs. Post your free job today to connect with top emerging talent for part-time roles

PARALLELS

A simple to use program that allows Mac users simply swipe their screen and start working in a full Windows environment. Now for $99/year you can have both machines on one. Very useful is you use a Mac at home and your office uses PCs.

PDF EDITOR

A great alternative and in some ways better than Adobe Acrobat. It costs a flat fee of $79.00 lifetime vs. $159.00/year for Adobe Acrobat. This is an amazing value. On your laptop you can edit, highlight, checkbox, sign, stamp, and perform other editing functions.

POCKET

This is a Chrome extension that allows you to bookmark any page you are viewing in a graphical way so that you can return to those pages and organize them for further viewing.

PODCASTS

Learn just about anything. I am amazed how few people take advantage of podcasts. They are in every possible topic. A recent one I heard was called "Presidential" which was 30-45 min podcasts of each President.   There are podcasts in every possible category.

RAKUTEN

Once you put install this on your computer, any site that supports discounts with Rakuten will automatically get you discounts. It actually works. You get rebate checks in the mail periodically.

READ (QX READ)

Medical journal article aggregator. This is surprisingly a knock-out product. You get summaries (the abstracts) of all the journals and/or journal topics you determine in your settings. A quick way to keep up with the literature.

With this app you can easily display your smartphone onto your computer screen to demonstrate how you use things.

SHASAM

The easiest to use app that identifies songs that you are listening to.

SHOW MY DESKTOP

This is an app that installs on your menu bar. By clicking on it hides all screens that are open immediately. Two good uses- if your boss walks by is one. The other is if you have so many windows open and you want to minimize them all in one keystroke.

Screen capture program. When you use this, you can capture not only any part of the screen and save it as an image, but you can create a movie based on your using the computer. This is called a screen recorder. This is a great way to demonstrate the use of software on your computer.

SPOTIFY

A very popular and powerful music streaming app.

TAPT.IO

A combination device and app. This is a metal business card that contains all your contact information as a replacement for a business card. When you tap a Smartphone, your contacts are transferred.

If you have a project at home, this is the app to find contractors or people who will assemble or clean anything you want. You have a task, you will find someone to do it for you with this.

THE SCORE

Sports app. A great dedicated app to find out sports scores in nearly every national and international sport. Also has some sports news but the scores feature is amazing.

TO DO

List making tool for Smartphone, tablets, and computers. If you are a list type of person, this is the app for you. Make and share lists on the fly. Even have group lists.

When you make videos, you may want to post them online but in your own special section
1. YouTube Channels- a free way to catalog your own videos and have people subscribe to your channel
2. Vimeo- a pay service with more features related to privacy. You can also charge for viewing your videos if you want.

VIVINO

Wine app. Takes a picture of the label, finds the wine, and tells you about the wine. There are a lot of wine apps.

VLC

Alternative movie playing program. Plays many more formats than other players.

VOICE MEMOS

Make voice memos on your smartphone. Simple dedicated app. Stores these memos and allows you to share them.

YOUMAIL

Transcribe your voice messages. This app takes away your need to listen to voice messages. It catalogs them and you can save the voice messages and share them. No similar apps do these things better than YouMail.

WAZE

Traffic app. If you are not using this, then you are probably still in traffic.

WONDERSHARE MOCKITT

A cloud-based app that easily allows you to produce Smartphone and tablet application mockups that you can then show to developers so that they can make exactly what you want.

WUNDERSHARE UNICONVERTER

An amazing app that allows you to convert one file format into another, download URLs from the internet and convert them into any file format.

WORLD CARD

List making tool for Smartphone, tablets, and computers. If you are a list type of person, this is the app for you. Make and share lists on the fly. Even have group lists.

X-MIND

A mind-mapping program where you can put all your ideas on a ever-growing diagram connecting what you are working on visually.

A uniquely powerful cloud-based document management system. You can give people links to a specific document that they can then view.

ZOOM

We all know Zoom. But did you know that with paid accounts you can:
1. Have unlimited users for unlimited amounts of time
2. Have people pre-register for your meeting to collect any information through a registration form that you develop
3. Run a webinar where only the panelists are shown and the others are viewers until you allow them to use their audio and video.

www.ingramcontent.com/pod-product-compliance
Lightning Source LLC
Chambersburg PA
CBHW061325250726
48657CB00003B/1043